Lucy Moore

God's Word for Messy People

31 Bible readings and reflections

BRF

1
Getting beyond the 'meh'

The Son is the image of the invisible God, the firstborn over all creation. For in him all things were created: things in heaven and on earth, visible and invisible, whether thrones or powers or rulers or authorities; all things have been created through him and for him. He is before all things, and in him all things hold together.

Jesus. How does that name make you feel? I'd love to be like Paul here, bubbling over with passion about him. But if I'm honest, my reaction is too often more like the 'meh' that pops up on social media: the lazy verbal equivalent of a shrug. I hear 'Jesus' so often! You do, when you belong to a church, don't you? And it's too easy to pretend to have the 'right' reaction.

Jesus stands for the truth. He claimed to be 'the truth', spoke the truth, lived the truth, rejoiced to see it in others and saved his harshest criticisms for hypocrites, for those who pretend. So we can be sure that he wants us to be honest with him as we read on, even when that makes us think something that startles or even shocks our conscious mind.

We're going to step out of the busyness of life and catch the vision of Jesus again through a month's worth of Bible passages. We'll explore the way he demonstrates the Messy Church values of creativity, hospitality, inclusivity and celebration. Perhaps, if we could become more like Jesus in who we are and in what we do, our world would be revolutionised by the church.

If Jesus made the invisible God visible 2,000 years ago, we can make the invisible Jesus visible today as we ourselves come closer to him. It's an enormous dream, almost as enormous as Paul's description of him here.

2
Don't bin it

'Here is my servant, whom I uphold, my chosen one in whom I delight; I will put my Spirit on him, and he will bring justice to the nations. He will not shout or cry out, or raise his voice in the streets. A bruised reed he will not break, and a smouldering wick he will not snuff out.'

Hundreds of years before Jesus was born, the prophet Isaiah described somebody chosen by God as his unique man of action, as someone who takes things that are a mess, that are damaged or dying, that someone else would give up on and throw away. The chosen person takes these things and brings about his new way of being human through them, always giving them a second chance, a new lease of life: the ultimate upcycler.

Perhaps the Jewish fishermen on Lake Galilee 2,000 years ago felt bruised and broken by God's apparent long absence from his people, by the savage Roman invaders of their country, by the religious leaders who were turning their vibrant faith into a set of elitist rules and rituals. Maybe they felt insignificant and unable to make a difference in the world. Then along came a young carpenter with laughter in his eyes and a sense of purpose they'd never seen in anyone else, someone who called them to come and join him on his adventure: how could they refuse?

Think of the number of times Jesus demonstrated a gentle chemistry of transformative justice, encountering someone bruised and broken by the powerful, restoring them to full human dignity and reinstating their reason for living. In each of these encounters, Jesus showed us how God sees every person beneath the labels other people have stuck on them.

Just as the creator God took the formless, empty, dark earth and created light, life, order and fruitfulness, so Jesus brought that same creative and redemptive power into every one of his encounters with people.

What creative gentleness, what gentle rebuilding of a just society can you bring into your encounters with other human beings today?

3
Spot the difference

As Jesus looked up, he saw the rich putting their gifts into the temple treasury. He also saw a poor widow put in two very small copper coins. 'Truly I tell you,' he said, 'this poor widow has put in more than all the others. All these people gave their gifts out of their wealth; but she out of her poverty put in all she had to live on.'

Artists see. Scientists, too. The first step for many scientists, young or old, is noticing the natural world. Musicians hear. Wine tasters slurp. Presumably, great parfumiers sense wonders through their noses. Creativity often springs from taking the time and space to observe what really is.

Jesus was a great creative observer. He immersed himself in being human, every sense fully alive. Even as he seemed to be whiling away time, he was keenly observing the world around him in the bustling city, seeing it not through the all-seeing eyes of God, as he was in human form with all its limitations, but with the full force of his intelligence, character, wisdom and discernment. Any one of his disciples could have observed the widow, but only Jesus noticed.

Thirty years of living alongside people in a family, a village and on building sites, with the Spirit of God prompting him at every turn to see what most of us miss, meant that Jesus was a skilled people-watcher, observer of the natural world, fully aware of the present moment.

Make space today to see what's really there. It's part of living life to the full.

4

Birdbrained

'Consider the ravens: they do not sow or reap, they have no storeroom or barn; yet God feeds them. And how much more valuable you are than birds! Who of you by worrying can add a single hour to your life? Since you cannot do this very little thing, why do you worry about the rest? Consider how the wild flowers grow. They do not labour or spin. Yet I tell you, not even Solomon in all his splendour was dressed like one of these.'

Maybe Jesus is with his friends on a sunny hillside, with Judas and Matthew fretting over the empty purse, James and John worrying how their dad's coping in the fishing boat without them, and Joanna asking whether there would be 13 or 5,000 thousand for supper tonight. Infuriatingly, Jesus lies back on the grass with a straw in his mouth and waves up vaguely at birds hanging out on the air currents, flying for the fun of it.

One of the topsy-turvy things about creativity is that it may have no point. There need be no reason to play, to make something out of nothing. It's not about doing something useful, earning money, putting food on the table or gaining popularity or admiration. It's about as far from materialism as you can get. Taking a sabbath rest once a week is ludicrous if life is simply about productivity.

Arguably, any act of creation is an act of faith – faith that we are more than just consumers, that there is more to being human than what we can get out of life. There need be no point, except to be fully human, to live in the gift of the present and to risk being open to the current of God's Spirit.

Prove you're human: do something pointlessly creative today.

5
To infinity and beyond

As the time approached for him to be taken up to heaven, Jesus resolutely set out for Jerusalem. And he sent messengers on ahead, who went into a Samaritan village to get things ready for him; but the people there did not welcome him, because he was heading for Jerusalem. When the disciples James and John saw this, they asked, 'Lord, do you want us to call fire down from heaven to destroy them?' But Jesus turned and rebuked them.

In Bognor Regis, you can join in the annual International Birdman event, when people fling themselves off the pier in their own design of self-propelled flying machine. It is bonkers and beautiful in its inventiveness and cheerful willingness to fail.

Being a pioneer can be risky. Failure is likely (especially if dressed as a skateboarding cow). Going back and starting again a different way takes courage, perseverance, stubbornness and grit. There is always some form of danger. It might only be a mild danger, such as losing face, looking stupid or losing money; or it could be, as it was for Jesus, danger of excruciating pain and a terrible death.

Jesus imagined the world as God wants it to be and acted on that vision. He didn't shy away from the risk of the path he'd chosen. Here, we see him setting out towards Jerusalem 'resolutely': he had made his decision and nothing would turn him back. He was like a diver who launches off the top board, giving himself no option for changing his mind.

Creativity can be about imagining what doesn't exist yet, seeing what could be and having the courage to turn the vision into action. It's the first step of a journey towards transformation. As we see raw materials in front of us, we can choose the safe option and let them lie or we can risk failure and attempt to make something from them.

Whenever Jesus met someone, his creative imagination saw them as they could be and he acted on that. When he saw the distress of the human race, he resolutely acted on that, despite knowing the great cost.

God, show me what risk means for me.

6

My word!

In the beginning was the Word, and the Word was with God, and the Word was God. He was with God in the beginning. Through him all things were made; without him nothing was made that has been made. In him was life, and that life was the light of all mankind. The light shines in the darkness, and the darkness has not overcome it.

If you yourself were reduced to one word, what would that word be? What is at the core of your life, motivation and reason for living? What lies at the root of your hopes and dreams? What's written on your heart?

Jesus was like a performance poet who not only speaks the words they have written, but also has them tattooed indelibly all over their skin, wears them woven into every item of clothing, lives them out in every action and demonstrates them in every breath they breathe, every expression that flits across their face, sleeping, waking, in any mood, at every moment of their life. The words describe the poet, while the poet lives by the poem. The poet is the poem; the poem is the poet.

Creativity is about expression, about communication. A photograph speaks in a different language from that of a piece of music, but each comes from the artist trying to communicate something of their inner vision. Usually, but not always, we expect to communicate with someone else, so creativity can often involve a relationship.

Jesus lived out the word of God. He was full of integrity; there was no room for anything not of God's word in his life. And that word spoke, communicated, expressed, could not help but create relationship: he spoke and listened to the creative word of God in every person he met.

What word will you speak out today?

7
Holy splurging

'Listen! A farmer went out to sow his seed. As he was scattering the seed, some fell along the path, and the birds came and ate it up. Some fell on rocky places, where it did not have much soil. It sprang up quickly, because the soil was shallow. But when the sun came up, the plants were scorched, and they withered because they had no root. Other seed fell among thorns, which grew up and choked the plants, so that they did not bear grain. Still other seed fell on good soil. It came up, grew and produced a crop, some multiplying thirty, some sixty, some a hundred times.'

Is it possible to be both miserly and creative? Can you give creative responses if you cannot bear to waste a thing? As a writer, I sometimes picture my thousands of deleted words, sentences, paragraphs slowly filling up a waste pit somewhere in cyberspace as I discard one phrase after another. I'm not an engineer, but I understand the process involves a certain amount of trial and error, creative thinking, throwing in far more ideas than are needed, in order to get past the obvious and into the better-quality solutions.

Creative people accept that the best outcome is impossible without waste, just as the farmer in Jesus' story does. Better outcomes take time and space to achieve and that time and space might feel or look like a waste. But for those in the know, they are an investment, a necessary part of the process. Jesus didn't charge straight to Calvary, but 'wasted' time in living, watching, learning, before sowing his vision of the kingdom with wild abandon in both dodgy and good ground.

Are you facing an empty field at the moment? How about 'wasting' some of your resources on it?

8

Play pays

[The teachers of the law and the Pharisees] said to Jesus, 'Teacher, this woman was caught in the act of adultery. In the Law Moses commanded us to stone such women. Now what do you say?' They were using this question as a trap, in order to have a basis for accusing him. But Jesus bent down and started to write on the ground with his finger. When they kept on questioning him, he straightened up and said to them, 'Let any one of you who is without sin be the first to throw a stone at her'... At this, those who heard began to go away one at a time, the older ones first, until only Jesus was left, with the woman still standing there. Jesus straightened up and asked her, 'Woman, where are they? Has no one condemned you?'

Why was Jesus looking down and doodling in the dust at this tense and crucial moment? Arguably, this was the moment when he saw clearly just how God's law was being manipulated for political ends to attack the vulnerable instead of protecting them.

He bent over and got back in touch with the dust of the earth that human beings come from. Like God's finger etching Moses' stone tablets, Jesus' finger was heaven touching earth, making a creative space for change.

Next time you explore God's word in a Messy activity, try to remember this moment: of downcast eyes, hands engaged in making something from the stuff of the earth, of space to think, to come up with questions and answers that cut to the truth, where heaven touches earth. It is play, transitory, wiped out in seconds, but play that brings life out of death, that can recreate human dignity and set old and young on to a new path that leads to life.

As you're out and about today, even if it feels daft, bend down and touch the ground in your office, school, street or home, and take a moment to remember the way Jesus bent down from heaven to earth and touched the life of our planet.

9
Yes to life!

'For John the Baptist came neither eating bread nor drinking wine, and you say, "He has a demon." The Son of Man came eating and drinking, and you say, "Here is a glutton and a drunkard, a friend of tax collectors and sinners."'

Was Jesus one of those people who wasn't really interested in food? He did fast in the desert and he seemed quite happy to go away all night without worrying about taking a snack with him. (Or maybe the disciples always made sure he had a sustaining sandwich or two in his pocket – we just don't know.)

I may be wrong, but I have an irrational feeling that he loved eating and drinking! Jesus was brought up in the glorious Jewish tradition of family meals and community festivals, after all – mealtimes would have had a resonance and vibrancy of shared community that must have meant they were something to look forward to. And mealtimes are by and large times he would have spent in the company of others, and Jesus adored being with other people. Mealtimes can mean thankfulness, togetherness, abundance, provision, community, acceptance, self-worth… They communicate way more than just food to fill us up.

Hospitality is an expression of the love of life itself, an affirmation of vitality, sustenance, community, something that lifts food above mere materialism and recognises its divine significance. When we invite others to our table or accept the invitation of others to eat together, we are saying 'yes!' to life, and no one said 'yes' to life louder than Jesus.

Celebrate what you're doing when you eat and drink today.

10
Pouring out hospitality

Now [Jesus] had to go through Samaria. So he came to a town in Samaria called Sychar, near the plot of ground Jacob had given to his son Joseph. Jacob's well was there, and Jesus, tired as he was from the journey, sat down by the well. It was about noon. When a Samaritan woman came to draw water, Jesus said to her, 'Will you give me a drink?' (His disciples had gone into the town to buy food.)

Rest, water, food. Jesus was very human and needed all three. (Ironically, there's no hint that he actually got any of them any time soon on this particular day!) We see him, in his human need, asking for hospitality from a very unlikely person, but the only person who was around. She was from a different culture; was of a different gender, in a time when gender divides were much clearer than they are in the west today; had a completely different way of life and a wildly different set of values. But Jesus grinned, accepted the Holy Spirit's timing and asked her for hospitality. There was a vulnerability about him that made space for the woman to be vulnerable in return.

If we are always the givers, the hosts to a needy world, do we run the risk of never admitting our own need of others and of never allowing others to flourish by contributing? Jesus could see the woman had so much to give, starting with the practical use of her water jar, but very quickly careering into the spiritual. He was willing to accept from her as well as pour out his riches to her. I do hope he got a drink somehow...

Lord, help us to enjoy receiving from others as well as giving out to them.

11

Bowels of compassion

A man with leprosy came to [Jesus] and begged him on his knees, 'If you are willing, you can make me clean.' Jesus was filled with compassion. He reached out his hand and touched the man. 'I am willing,' he said. 'Be clean!' Immediately the leprosy left him and he was cleansed.

What do people want and need from their local church? What state of mind are they in as they approach the doors or stray on to the Facebook page? And what is in the minds of the church's gatekeepers as they prepare services, stand at the door on the welcome team, decide what to prioritise and work out the church's vision?

Part of true hospitality is an attitude that reaches out creatively, imaginatively towards others. It's an empathy that gets inside their skin, walks in their shoes, sees through their eyes, feels their needs, joys or pain. Jesus was supernaturally good at this – at great personal cost. In this encounter, he didn't just understand in his head what the man with leprosy was going through; he felt it in his gut. It was visceral, life-changing, painful and drove him to immediate action.

Hospitality reaches out in compassion towards another human being and lets us experience something of what they are going through. Messy Church began, after all, partly because of feeling the pain of families unable to join in church worship. And, whether we're standing at a church door welcoming people in or encountering people at work or at home, we need to keep making ourselves humble and vulnerable enough to listen and ensure what we are offering as a church and as individuals continues to meet the needs of the people God puts in front of us.

Picture some situation you're in today from the other person's standpoint.

12

Magnetic attraction

The acts of the flesh are obvious: sexual immorality, impurity and debauchery; idolatry and witchcraft; hatred, discord, jealousy, fits of rage, selfish ambition, dissensions, factions and envy; drunkenness, orgies, and the like. I warn you, as I did before, that those who live like this will not inherit the kingdom of God. But the fruit of the Spirit is love, joy, peace, forbearance, kindness, goodness, faithfulness, gentleness and self-control.

I've met some amazing people over the years – particularly in this Messy Church network – who have exhibited so many qualities from the second list and have been such a joy to be with. And I want to be with them. I want to visit them again, spend time enjoying their company, have my difficulties soothed by their love and patience, and have the rough sides of me gently rubbed smooth by their wisdom, generosity and acceptance. There are so many people I want to be like!

As we apprentice ourselves to Christ, becoming more and more like him, both as individuals and as a church, we will become more attractive to others. If we love and enjoy life, demonstrate peace, forbearance and forgiveness, treat those less powerful than ourselves with kindness and gentleness, and have an integrity that keeps body and soul unified, people will want to hang out with us and find the way of life that helps us live as we do. Our character will be a vital part of our hospitality.

Pick a fruit for today and be more… fruity.

13
Nerf gun, anyone?

When Jesus had finished speaking, a Pharisee invited him to eat with him; so he went in and reclined at the table. But the Pharisee was surprised when he noticed that Jesus did not first wash before the meal. Then the Lord said to him, 'Now then, you Pharisees clean the outside of the cup and dish, but inside you are full of greed and wickedness. You foolish people! Did not the one who made the outside make the inside also? But now as for what is inside you – be generous to the poor, and everything will be clean for you.'

One aspect of hospitality that we wrestle with in our Messy Church is setting boundaries. A good host has boundaries for what is acceptable and maintains the integrity of the establishment or community so that everyone can be safe and happy. Workplaces have an ethos of how to behave; my son discovered to his glee that Nerf gun battles happen regularly in his new office, though his previous employers would have within milliseconds sacked anyone with anything ballistic about their person.

While these 'rules' can be a helpful way of stating what a particular community stands for, they may also be abused as a way of keeping out people who 'don't belong'. Was this Pharisee really concerned about the safety and well-being of his household, when he showed his shock at Jesus' lack of observation of the ceremonial washing practice? Or was he more concerned to find fault with Jesus, to prove that he really wasn't 'one of us'?

Integrity in our hospitality needs some careful thought, in order to balance the aims of our community with the needs of guests and our own hidden motivation.

14
Revolutionary hospitality

An argument started among the disciples as to which of them would be the greatest. Jesus, knowing their thoughts, took a little child and made him stand beside him. Then he said to them, 'Whoever welcomes this little child in my name welcomes me; and whoever welcomes me welcomes the one who sent me. For it is the one who is least among you all who is the greatest.'

For more of a feel for what Jesus was saying to a very different culture, picture this scene differently: instead of Jesus taking a child, imagine Jesus taking someone with a mental disability. Or a slightly smelly rough sleeper. Or a traumatised asylum seeker. Or someone with dementia… whoever your culture sees as an economic drain on resources, who – some claim – has no 'use', who makes no contribution, who is easily exploited.

What are you doing when you welcome 'these little children' to your church? You are participating in a revolutionary act of defiance that hurls a challenge to the forces of materialism and consumerism that hold so much power today. You are on the barricades with your weapons of glue guns, icing nozzles and bulk purchases of frozen peas. You are championing a different way of life, the kingdom way of life, where every human being is beautiful and precious in God's sight and is to be honoured by Jesus' people, to show the world that there is a better way and that it works.

The early church ate together, shocking their rigid society by the implication that in the church, all are equal, whether slaves or free. Our mealtime says something very similar without words as we sit down with people from all walks of life.

Jesus, build your kingdom, table by table.

15
Chicken wings

'Jerusalem, Jerusalem, you who kill the prophets and stone those sent to you, how often I have longed to gather your children together, as a hen gathers her chicks under her wings, and you were not willing. Look, your house is left to you desolate. I tell you, you will not see me again until you say, "Blessed is he who comes in the name of the Lord."'

Now that my children have grown up and spread themselves around the country, I long for those special times – Christmas, Easter, holidays – when they all come back to see us. They are times of special meals, of special treats, of catching up and enjoying the sense of being together. And yes, of course, we would drive each other demented if they never went away again; but for that brief time we have together, it's time to party.

Jesus' longing for the togetherness of family was even greater and more profound. Here, at the end of a chapter about confrontation and kingdom, he pours out his heart about his love for God's people and his yearning for them to scuttle into the safety and warmth of their rightful relationship with God, like chicks rushing towards their mother. But, tragically, 'you were not willing'.

As we become more like Jesus, our longings start to match his longings. Our motivation is less and less about wanting to see personal success, greater numbers in our church or proving to everyone that we were right after all. Instead, we long for people's well-being as Jesus does, out of heartfelt love.

Hospitality is about creating a loving sanctuary where people can thrive and grow and feel safe, where they can come home and where the party never ends.

Put the name of your village, town or city into Jesus' words, instead of 'Jerusalem'.

16

Joining in

When Jesus had called the Twelve together, he gave them power and authority to drive out all demons and to cure diseases, and he sent them out to proclaim the kingdom of God and to heal those who were ill... After this the Lord appointed seventy-two others and sent them two by two ahead of him to every town and place where he was about to go.

Jesus was generous. He shared everything he had, including his vision and his mission, and he invited everyone to join in. First, the twelve got the chance to go on an adventure, then the 72. Then, after the day of Pentecost, it's an open invitation to all who believe in him, regardless of nationality, previous faith group, gender or age: young, old, men, women, as Joel had said it would be on the day of the Lord some centuries before (see Joel 2:28). Some radical plans take a long time to come to fruition!

Up to then, only the big boys were able to play; now the field was open to everyone. In each generation, we need to fight to give back to the voiceless their rightful place in the mission of Jesus. When people are excluded because of gender, background, race, education or age, we are given the chance to go back to ancient ways and make the church as inclusive as Jesus meant it to be.

Messy Church is part of this pattern of recalibrating churches. The very old are honoured and welcomed and have a purpose, and it's the same for the very young and everyone in between, regardless of gender or background. In fact, 'everyone who calls on the name of the Lord' (Joel 2:32) has a vital role to play in growing the kingdom through their local church.

Is anyone calling on the name of the Lord near you who hasn't yet found a place of belonging in your church?

17
Everyone's ideas, please!

When Jesus had entered Capernaum, a centurion came to him, asking for help. 'Lord,' he said, 'my servant lies at home paralysed, suffering terribly.' Jesus said to him, 'Shall I come and heal him?' The centurion replied, 'Lord, I do not deserve to have you come under my roof. But just say the word, and my servant will be healed. For I myself am a man under authority, with soldiers under me...' When Jesus heard this, he was amazed and said to those following him, 'Truly I tell you, I have not found anyone in Israel with such great faith...' Then Jesus said to the centurion, 'Go! Let it be done just as you believed it would.' And his servant was healed at that moment.

This outsider really shouldn't have understood anything about the way God works and, frankly, should have been ignored. Spiritually, this centurion must surely have been a complete ignoramus, mustn't he? How could he know anything about the true God when he belonged to a nation of false gods? Imagine how the Jewish listeners were feeling.

But his reply to Jesus' question left Jesus amazed at the centurion's insight. Jesus suddenly saw him not just as a human being in need of compassion, but also as a sign of the opening of the kingdom to people outside the Jewish faith. He even changed his plans to honour the centurion's response.

Being an all-age, inclusive faith community requires us to be receptive when unexpected people express their insights into the things of God. It might mean changing what we were going to do, when, perhaps, children or people with a different belief framework or set of values from our own make suggestions. It requires humility and discernment to sense whether God may be challenging us through their words. But if Jesus could do it, we can.

Make a point today of listening to someone you would normally avoid or ignore.

18

Allsorts

As [Jesus] walked along, he saw Levi son of Alphaeus sitting at the tax collector's booth. 'Follow me,' Jesus told him, and Levi got up and followed him. While Jesus was having dinner at Levi's house, many tax collectors and sinners were eating with him and his disciples, for there were many who followed him. When the teachers of the law who were Pharisees saw him eating with the sinners and tax collectors, they asked his disciples: 'Why does he eat with tax collectors and sinners?' On hearing this, Jesus said to them, 'It is not the healthy who need a doctor, but those who are ill. I have not come to call the righteous, but sinners.'

What were Jesus' disciples thinking as they lay down around Levi's table? These fellow-guests were the sort of folk a nice Jewish fisherman's parents would have warned him to stay away from, and who would almost certainly incur foot-tapping from that fisherman's wife. The disciples hadn't been with Jesus very long, after all: did they trust him not to lead them into dissolute ways among these people, who weren't quite our sort? I mean, a tax collector – a tax collector! And that man leaning across for the mustard, who usually makes you cross the street rather than go anywhere near him… What sort of kingdom was this? What sort of leader was Jesus if he couldn't see who these people were?

Any time we find ourselves wishing somebody wasn't there at church, Messy or otherwise, we need to remember this story and ask ourselves what we're here for, *who* we're here for. Jesus came for everyone, not just nice, sorted people (as if any of us are). He actively sought and enjoyed the company of people who weren't perfect. He laid himself, his reputation and his disciples down to make a way for everyone to find their way back to God.

Acknowledge any false sense of superiority in yourself towards someone else, and ask Jesus for his forgiveness.

19

The usefulness of others

Then people brought little children to Jesus for him to place his hands on them and pray for them. But the disciples rebuked them. Jesus said, 'Let the little children come to me, and do not hinder them, for the kingdom of heaven belongs to such as these.' When he had placed his hands on them, he went on from there.

Somebody exclaimed smilingly to me, 'You like children, don't you?' I was a little uncomfortable. 'I like *some* children,' I said. 'Some, I can't stand. A bit like how I feel about adults, really.' Perhaps I was being unfair. Adults have had more time to make decisions about who they want to be and aspire to be and have had the chance to work on their character. Children are still finding out who they are and who they want to become.

In this encounter, Jesus went way beyond liking or disliking these particular children. He affirmed the right of people of all ages to come close to him. He gave the powerful adults a sharp reminder of the way the kingdom of God should operate, with access to God for everyone, not just the few chosen men. And he affirmed and articulated the children's citizenship of the kingdom, along with the poor in spirit and the persecuted.

When we are an intergenerational church, we have a constant reminder that it's not 'all about me'. We are constantly challenged to make allowances for 'the weaker brethren' of whatever age and to serve rather than expect to be served. We are constantly challenged to face the fact that God wants people other than ourselves to be close to him and to receive his blessing.

How can you be a blessing today to someone of a different age from your own?

20

Storykeepers

There was also a prophet, Anna, the daughter of Penuel, of the tribe of Asher. She was very old; she had lived with her husband seven years after her marriage, and then was a widow until she was eighty-four. She never left the temple but worshipped night and day, fasting and praying. Coming up to them at that very moment, she gave thanks to God and spoke about the child to all who were looking forward to the redemption of Jerusalem.

An intergenerational church is one that treasures its older people as well as its younger ones. There's an argument within generational theory that one generation can be of particular help to another specific generation. For instance, the world views of baby boomers (born 1943–60) and millennials (born

1982–2004) resonate in many ways, so millennials are more likely to appreciate mentoring from the boomer generation than from Generation X (born 1961–81). In other words, my young adult children are likely to find the mentoring of someone from my mother's or grandmother's generation more helpful than that of someone from my generation. We need each other.

An intergenerational church expects to be together, to value each other, to need each other and to help each other to enjoy life in all its fullness. The baby Jesus gave to the older woman, Anna, the vindication of a life lived for God and hope for the future of her people. Anna gave Mary and Joseph the reassurance of Jesus' identity under God from her perspective of advanced age and accumulated spiritual wisdom, and she did her bit to pave the way for Jesus' adult ministry, although she would not be there to enjoy it.

What friendships can you promote safely across the generations in your church?

21

Get out of the way!

[Jesus] said to them, 'Why are you thinking these things? Which is easier: to say to this paralysed man, "Your sins are forgiven," or to say, "Get up, take your mat and walk"? But I want you to know that the Son of Man has authority on earth to forgive sins.' So he said to the man, 'I tell you, get up, take your mat and go home.' He got up, took his mat and walked out in full view of them all. This amazed everyone and they praised God, saying, 'We have never seen anything like this!'

People got in the way of the man on the mat so that he couldn't get to Jesus. Nobody said, 'He needs Jesus more than I do – I'll give up my place in the room so that he can get through.' Nobody offered to pass the mat over the heads of the crowd. It was left to the dogged determination of his friends and their roof-dismantling abilities to get their friend to where he needed to be. Once he was in contact with Jesus, he received healing inside and out and became a new source of amazement and reason for praising God. Until then, he'd just been considered a nuisance.

We sometimes need to make sacrifices in order to enable other people to come closer to Jesus. The people in this crowd had every spiritual justification for wanting to be as close to Jesus as possible, but they prevented someone more needy from reaching him. For us, we might be holding on to something equally justifiable and spiritual: a style of singing or praying; a need for silence or for volume; the timing of a service; a style of service that requires a particular leader to be present, taking them away from others. It's worth examining whether any of these might be preventing someone else approaching Jesus and, if so, whether we are prepared to give it up gracefully, believing that seeing God at work in the life of another may make it all worth it.

Ask your church leader if they think there is any way in which you could be helping someone else come closer to Jesus.

22

Including… excluding…

Jesus went up on a mountainside and called to him those he wanted, and they came to him. He appointed twelve that they might be with him and that he might send them out to preach and to have authority to drive out demons. These are the twelve he appointed: Simon (to whom he gave the name Peter); James son of Zebedee and his brother John (to them he gave the name Boanerges, which means 'sons of thunder'), Andrew, Philip, Bartholomew, Matthew, Thomas, James son of Alphaeus, Thaddaeus, Simon the Zealot and Judas Iscariot, who betrayed him.

When Mark wrote his gospel, this exclusively male list of apostles may well have raised no eyebrows, but it does today. We know from other mentions in the gospels that Jesus had female disciples too, so why are none of them appointed here? It can only be conjecture, but we could say that Jesus knew he had to work within the constraints of his culture while paving the way for a more inclusive future. He had such a huge plan, so massive in the scope of change it involved, that it couldn't happen overnight. He deliberately limited himself to what that society could handle, one step at a time.

Sadly, though, all too often through the centuries the church has downplayed, distorted and almost lost the significance of women as equally loved and valued disciples of Christ. How will history judge us as a church? Will we be the ones to play it safe and go with what 'the church' has always done, or will we be faithful to Jesus' world-shaking vision of a kingdom of equality, where the old dividing lines are rubbed out?

Who gets downplayed in our chapter of God's story?

23
The great escape

[Jesus] stood up to read, and the scroll of the prophet Isaiah was handed to him. Unrolling it, he found the place where it is written: 'The Spirit of the Lord is on me, because he has anointed me to proclaim good news to the poor. He has sent me to proclaim freedom for the prisoners and recovery of sight for the blind, to set the oppressed free, to proclaim the year of the Lord's favour.' Then he rolled up the scroll, gave it back to the attendant and sat down. The eyes of everyone in the synagogue were fastened on him. He began by saying to them, 'Today this scripture is fulfilled in your hearing.'

There is so much to celebrate! The very reason Jesus came wasn't to bring judgement and condemnation leading to prison sentences, but to set people free from everything that stops them living life in all its fullness. Jesus' whole purpose was to bring freedom. He spent his three years opening doors and windows for people to escape from limitations, expectations, reputations and obfuscation – a work that came to a cosmic fulfilment on the cross when he set God's people free once and for all.

Being a Christian is about stepping out day by day into more and more freedom and showing other people how to find that freedom for themselves. Each Messy Church session is an invitation to escape from the dingy cell of materialism, criticism, hunger, despair, loneliness and apathy, and to take a step towards the light together. It's a celebration of who Jesus is and what he's done for us, story by story, as the light of freedom grows brighter.

As you prepare your next work for God, whatever it may be, take a moment to see yourself as the head of the Escape Committee, shining the torch to show the way out.

24
Party faith

'Or suppose a woman has ten silver coins and loses one. Doesn't she light a lamp, sweep the house and search carefully until she finds it? And when she finds it, she calls her friends and neighbours together and says, "Rejoice with me; I have found my lost coin." In the same way, I tell you, there is rejoicing in the presence of the angels of God over one sinner who repents.'

Apparently, I have a very distinctive laugh. It pops out in public occasionally, to my embarrassment, especially when it happens somewhere like in a cathedral. Upbubblings of joy aren't terribly English and are met with disapproval, especially in church – which might be why children have found it so difficult to belong to churches, when they haven't learned to control their joy yet and their glee is met with a 'Shh!'. Do you ever feel embarrassed about the fun, laughter or exuberant joy of the church you belong to? I mean, can it really be church if people are enjoying themselves so much? How quickly we want to get everyone on to the 'real' issues of guilt, repentance, cost, pain and suffering, thoughts of which elicit far more 'appropriate' solemn, churchy responses.

But Jesus shone a light here on a heavenly perspective, which is one of joy, glee and uninhibited community partying based on something real and wonderful to celebrate. People are coming home to God! If the ground state of our churches is one of joy, people will naturally want to join in. They will be swept in willy-nilly. The celebration itself will speak more of God's plan than any carefully worded theology. Partying is at the heart of our faith and we can rejoice in that truth – and laugh!

Count up the instances of laughter next time you gather as a church or home group. How delighted are you with the result?

25

A God to celebrate

[Jesus said,] 'Now my soul is troubled, and what shall I say? "Father, save me from this hour"? No, it was for this very reason I came to this hour. Father, glorify your name!' Then a voice came from heaven, 'I have glorified it, and will glorify it again.' The crowd that was there and heard it said it had thundered; others said an angel had spoken to him.

Jesus lived to 'glorify God's name'. In practice, he interpreted that as demonstrating to people how much God loves them and then demonstrating total obedience and trust in God by going to the cross to die. His words, actions and decisions had that singlemindedness of 'glorifying God's name'. Jesus celebrated God every moment of his life and in every atom of his being. He lived and died in celebration of his Father. His vision, purpose, mission, actions and words came across with an unsurpassed power of integrity: he simply lived to glorify, to celebrate God.

I wonder what exactly it was about God that Jesus delighted in? Was it the intricacy of the unfolding of God's plan that Jesus saw in scripture? Was it God's heart of bottomless compassion? Was it Jesus' own place in God's designs that he rejoiced in? What delights you about God? Why do you want to share this aspect of God with others?

If life seems disjointed and piecemeal at the moment, try taking time today to remind yourself of the big picture. When it comes to the crunch, what matters? If you peel everything else away, what is your life all about? What is your church there for?

How will you simply celebrate or 'glorify' God in your thoughts, actions and words today?

26

Neighbours to celebrate

A woman came with an alabaster jar of very expensive perfume... She broke the jar and poured the perfume on [Jesus'] head. Some of those present were saying indignantly to one another, 'Why this waste of perfume? It could have been sold for more than a year's wages and the money given to the poor'... 'Leave her alone,' said Jesus. 'Why are you bothering her? She has done a beautiful thing to me. The poor you will always have with you, and you can help them any time you want. But you will not always have me. She did what she could. She poured perfume on my body beforehand to prepare for my burial. Truly I tell you, wherever the gospel is preached throughout the world, what she has done will also be told, in memory of her.'

One of the most attractive things about Jesus is that he actually likes people. This might not seem remarkable, but it is! I think of my own shortcomings, including (to my shame) finding it much easier to like ideas (so safe! so controllable!) than to like people (so unpredictable! so inconsistent!), and I compare myself to Jesus, and whimper.

Jesus delighted in the woman pouring perfume. He celebrated what the woman had done and set it in a context of eternal significance. He didn't care what everyone else at the table thought. He celebrated the woman and her silent, extravagant, wholehearted action.

In Messy Church, we often have the opportunity to celebrate people, to affirm them as significant members of the community. Every meal we provide, every genuine moment of listening, every word of appreciation reflects Jesus' celebration of this woman 2,000 years ago, who is still remembered today.

Which one person can you celebrate today with a word or email that lets them know how significant they are?

27

More than being nice to your sister

At that time Jesus, full of joy through the Holy Spirit, said, 'I praise you, Father, Lord of heaven and earth, because you have hidden these things from the wise and learned, and revealed them to little children. Yes, Father, for this is what you were pleased to do.'

Look at Jesus here, celebrating God as he saw the kingdom of heaven happening before his eyes in the excitement of the disciples coming back to him, full of stories of God at work. It's a moment of pure joy, pure insight, pure worship. It's a moment when he articulates the revelation of a mystery and of the character of God. It's also one of those rare moments in the gospels when Jesus' feelings are described unambiguously. He was 'full of joy'. When did the vision of God at work, either in his word or in the world around you, last make you 'full of joy'?

We still suffer in church from an outdated way of teaching that says, 'And the meaning of the story is…', usually ending with 'Jesus wants you to tidy your room', 'Don't tell lies' or 'Be nice to your sister.' Awesome Bible stories, puzzling Bible stories and disturbing Bible stories are reduced to morality tales instead of being allowed to be doorways to mystery. You would have thought, with all the wonderful influence of the Godly Play movement on spiritual formation, that it would be enough to open up the story rather than feeling we need to provide 'the meaning' of it, dictating the application of a Bible story as if we knew best, as if there is a single meaning. What happens when we simply make space to celebrate the story?

Jesus, help me to delight in God as you did. Help me to relish the unknowable as well as the knowing.

28

Down to the bone

'And when you pray, do not keep on babbling like pagans, for they think they will be heard because of their many words. Do not be like them, for your Father knows what you need before you ask him. This, then, is how you should pray: "Our Father in heaven, hallowed be your name, your kingdom come, your will be done, on earth as it is in heaven. Give us today our daily bread. And forgive us our debts, as we also have forgiven our debtors. And lead us not into temptation, but deliver us from the evil one."'

Sometimes we don't feel like celebrating. We don't feel like celebrating who God is, who our neighbours are, the intricacies of God's word or indeed anything: the 'meh' of apathy described in our very first reading threatens to sap all the energy from our faith.

Jesus was well aware of how human beings work, experiencing the fun-filled festivals and the pedestrian plod of living out faith. As a practising Jew, he had set prayers and practices as well as spontaneous outbursts of worship. Perhaps he sometimes didn't feel like keeping up with his prayer times. Perhaps he was the one human being who loved them 100% of the time. He certainly understood that the rest of us sometimes find it hard to keep going with faith.

How do we celebrate when we don't feel celebratory? This is when the simple disciplines of a disciple's life come into play, those unglamorous routines that hold us firm, like a skeleton, when the surrounding flesh threatens to wobble off course. Rituals are a vital part of a healthy life. Prayers like the Lord's Prayer can be said from the inside out but also from the outside in when the going is tough.

If you find yourself about to say or do something negative today, pause, count to three and say instead, 'Your kingdom come.'

29
Safe celebration

Jesus spoke to them again in parables, saying: 'The kingdom of heaven is like a king who prepared a wedding banquet for his son... So the servants went out into the streets and gathered all the people they could find, the bad as well as the good, and the wedding hall was filled with guests. But when the king came in to see the guests, he noticed a man there who was not wearing wedding clothes. He asked, "How did you get in here without wedding clothes, friend?" The man was speechless. Then the king told the attendants, "Tie him hand and foot, and throw him outside, into the darkness, where there will be weeping and gnashing of teeth." For many are invited, but few are chosen.'

On the one hand, the king in today's parable pushed the boat out with wild abandon. He prepared stacks of food, gave out invitations indiscriminately and threw open the doors. It's a great celebration, a wonderful openhanded free-for-all. On the other hand, it's not. There were boundaries. There were expectations of behaviour, of what was appropriate to wear and what was simply rude. The exuberance of the king's generosity was matched by his over-the-top punishment when a guest crossed the line.

Where are the boundaries in our churches? How do we make a safe space not just for welcoming people in but for the transformation of actions, habits and character? Do we love people enough to want the very best for them or are we content with 'anything goes' as long as they come in through the door?

Are we prepared to communicate the tough side of following Jesus as well as the fun?

30
Messy life

'I have come that they may have life, and have it to the full.'

An addict finds God and stops taking heroin, becoming a leader of addiction courses on the local estate. An older woman finds company and friendship in her isolated life. Two young people meet and get married. Teenagers get respite from having to be grown up too soon. A leader discovers what it means to need other people in the team. A mother and her daughter explore how to pray. A family is fed when the food has run out over the weekend.

Messy Churches have played a part in all these gentle, real-life stories of life in all its fullness, and in many more that are too personal to be shared publicly. Churches have found their childless arms full to overflowing with young life. 'Our problem is space now: our building isn't big enough to do it safely.'

Jesus lived to give. He lived to give his life to God and to the people God loves. He lives on now through his Holy Spirit in each of us, giving us life and inviting us to make a space where others can find that overflowing life for themselves.

Where Jesus is at the centre of every planning meeting, activity table, celebration and meal table, his life will inevitably overflow into ours. His Holy Spirit will call out from one heart to another, bringing us closer to each other in word, sacrament, play, worship, food and laughter.

I poured the drinks last night at Messy Church. The water jug was very full and sloshed all over the table, my plate, my lap and the floor. The children at my table thought it was hysterical. It was certainly messy. A smaller, emptier jug would have been tidier, but… Spend a moment letting a bowl or jug overflow under a running tap. How much is it similar to or dissimilar to your own life at the moment?

31
Messy hamsters?

Then I saw 'a new heaven and a new earth,' for the first heaven and the first earth had passed away, and there was no longer any sea. I saw the Holy City... coming down out of heaven from God, prepared as a bride beautifully dressed for her husband. And I heard a loud voice from the throne saying, 'Look! God's dwelling-place is now among the people, and he will dwell with them. They will be his people, and God himself will be with them and be their God. "He will wipe every tear from their eyes. There will be no more death" or mourning or crying or pain, for the old order of things has passed away.'

What are we doing? Every month, we turn up, welcome, smile, encourage, listen, chat, wonder, cook, wipe up, clear up, scrape up, wash up, sweep up. Then plan the next one. Is it a hamster wheel of never-ending busyness so that at least our generation can look as if we tried?

No. These actions are just the outward appearances of an inner reality. What is happening is something far more profound than a jolly once-a-month carnival. Every Messy Church is opening a window on to this vision of John's, which says there is more to life than what we see here and now. We are being the kingdom that Jesus died to bring about. We're feeding the hungry and bringing light into dark places, setting prisoners free and telling God's story afresh for a new generation. We are opening the door for Jesus to come in and eat with us.

When I look at the photos of the many Messy Churches on Facebook, when I see the faces of the team members who turn up for training, when I look at my own team, I see the kingdom of justice and joy alive and well. I see old and young pioneering together to make it happen. I see laughter, unity, food and love. I see a new heaven and a new earth happening right here.

Have you ever helped a friend get ready for their wedding? Stand back and enjoy the chaos of your next Messy Church. If this is the changing room where the bride of Christ is getting ready, no wonder it's chaotic. It's a place of life, beauty, celebration and love.

The Bible Reading Fellowship
15 The Chambers, Vineyard
Abingdon OX14 3FE
brf.org.uk

The Bible Reading Fellowship (BRF) is a Registered Charity (233280)

ISBN 978 0 85746 749 2
First published 2019
10 9 8 7 6 5 4 3 2 1 0
All rights reserved

Text by Lucy Moore 2019
This edition © The Bible Reading Fellowship 2019
Cover and inside illustrations by Rebecca J Hall

The author asserts the moral right to be identified as the author of this work

Acknowledgements
Scripture quotations are from The Holy Bible, New International Version (Anglicised
edition) copyright © 1979, 1984, 2011 by Biblica. Used by permission of Hodder &
Stoughton Publishers, a Hachette UK company. All rights reserved. 'NIV' is a registered
trademark of Biblica. UK trademark number 1448790.

Every effort has been made to trace and contact copyright owners for material used
in this resource. We apologise for any inadvertent omissions or errors, and would
ask those concerned to contact us so that full acknowledgement can be made in
the future.

A catalogue record for this book is available from the British Library

Printed by Gutenberg Press, Tarxien, Malta